Buying The Dream:

DON'T GET STUCK WITH A NIGHTMARE

A Brief Compilation Of Things To Do
Before Purchasing Property

Victoria Williams

authorHOUSE®

AuthorHouse™
1663 Liberty Drive
Bloomington, IN 47403
www.authorhouse.com
Phone: 1 (800) 839-8640

Published by AuthorHouse 10/04/2017

ISBN: 978-1-5462-0887-7 (sc)
ISBN: 978-1-5462-0886-0 (e)

Library of Congress Control Number: 2017914384

Print information available on the last page.

This book is printed on acid-free paper.

Contents

FOREWORD

The twenty first century giant leap forward with technology and every bit of information available to anyone is a wonderful thing for the world of real estate, building and development. Television will show you how to design, decorate, flip for profit or just have fun spending money in real estate. All of this information has made many more people believe they can do it all on their own. Save a few dollars here, cut a corner there and you are so smart you saw it on television.

The number of amateurs in the real estate world just muddies the water with more amateur mistakes and hazards. Those hazards can cost thousands more than the advice and expertise of the right professional. Is this town's commercial zoning exactly like the town where you grew up? What about the zone rules in the town that is on the opposite side of the street? Does a fence determine the property line? Is the setback measured from structure to structure or from the drip line of the eave?

In this book, Victoria Williams lays out examples and warnings of why you should not swim in the world of real estate without hiring the right experts to protect you from the amateurs, politicians, regulators, and the self interest motivated. The cost of a Realtor can save thousands more than their commission in negotiating, contract review, historical, political, and building knowledge. The cost of hiring an architect who is a zoning and permit expert is dirt cheap compared to buying property by the truck load. Surveyors, building inspectors, architects, and other consultants do more transactions a year than you will do in a lifetime. That lifetime experience for hire is a bargain compared to the mistakes you could pay for without them. Victoria Williams has proven she's there to guide, protect, and provide her client with a better design experience.

Acknowledgements

Writing this book was not on my radar until Fabienne Fredrickson told me that I needed to put something out there to help those that don't know what they don't know. I thank her, Derek, Joe, Jodi, Emma, and everyone else at Boldheart for pushing me, believing in me, and holding me accountable.

I thank Pat Sabiston for her ongoing friendship, guidance, and editing talent. She inspires me daily.

Much thanks and love to Kim Griffin White for the amazing cover design and all of the vision and talent that she gives to her clients. Kim is as dynamic as her beautiful work.

Thank you to Teresa Tuno for the use of the head shot for the book. She is able to bring out the light that is within her clientele.

A huge thank you is extended to John Shook for writing the Forward for this book as well as for telling it like it is and always making sure that others have the information they need to make quality decisions.

I thank God for the strength and guidance He provides to me daily. I pray this book is a blessing to its readers.

Finally, a loving thank you to my sweet family, Todd, Morgan, and Ashtyn, for their encouragement and to the VBA Team for always providing, and delivering, a better experience not only to our clients, but to each other.

INTRODUCTION

I love my clients, I really do! When I meet them for the first time, and hear about their goals, dreams, and aspirations, I begin to see a glimpse of who they are as a person and what they value. When we take the journey together, I see their deepest desires and walk through the spaces in their mind, experiencing each one with the awe and anticipation of the possibility of bringing their thoughts into reality. It isn't, and will never be, about me or what I want them to have. Instead, it will always be about pulling this inner passion and vision out of their hearts and minds, building on it one piece at a time. The look on their face as they see this structure taking form, which they have so many times envisioned, but could not explain, is priceless and a true gift to encounter. This is the reason I do what I do.

However, there are other times when I must impart information to my clients that hurts them. It hurts their heart, future plans, dreams, and finances. I have seen their faces go from a bright, excited smile to tears. It is unbearable, but often preventable. This is the reason I feel this book must be written. I feel compelled to shed a light on those ugly, yet preventable, mistakes made by many when purchasing a piece of property without the knowledge of what to look for, and the tests needed prior to signing on the dotted line. Many buildings never reach their intended form due to "unforeseen site conditions." Don't get me wrong, we cannot do enough due diligence to envision every possible scenario, but there are steps which can be taken to minimize these issues. This is the intent of this book, to make life, and the building process, stress and error free.

Throughout these pages, you will find several pitfalls that have actually occurred and are not so farfetched. I share these experiences in order to provide you with a checklist of things to inspect, test, and research in order to select the correct site to enable you to build the structure of your dreams. There is an upfront investment to perform these tasks, but believe me, you will save time, money, and loads of stress in the long run by saying "no" to the wrong site and "yes" to the correct one. This exercise is a process. It isn't quick, nor easy. But, when you walk into your building, look around, take a deep breath and say "This is my space and it is exactly what I dreamed of," it will definitely be worth it.

YOUR SITE HAS BAGGAGE

I walk into the room observing my smiling, giggling clients sitting at the conference room table eagerly awaiting the presentation of the design documents for their dream home. It is clear their anticipation and excitement is incredibly high, and they have waited and dreamed of this moment for quite some time. I take a deep breath, sit down, and look into their eyes, knowing the news I am about to impart will immediately remove the wind from their sails.

"The geotechnical report shows your soils are unsuitable for the construction of your home. This will require us to use a pile foundation, or excavate the unsuitable soils, bring in fill, and surcharge the site for three months in order to be sure of the settlement that is expected of this site."

The smiles fade, shock sets in, and confusion reigns. In plain English, bad soils equal time and money. The budget is usually tight; time is of the essence since they are renting an apartment with an expiring lease; and they are faced with the possibility of not being able to afford to build their dream home. What now?

Initially, the lot had looked perfect to them with its gentle slope towards the bay, deep water access, enough water frontage for their boat and a rather nice dock, as well as ample acreage to build a beautiful, four-bedroom, three-bathroom, three-car garage home. The price was right for the lot and left enough wiggle room to enable them to get just enough financing to build their home, with the dock planned at a later date. Unfortunately, they fell in love with the lot prior to making sure their vision was able to become a reality. The lot had issues, not to mention "baggage."

The situation I just outlined is not uncommon. Many buyers function under the "location, location, location" adage without taking into consideration that there may be issues that are not conducive to meeting their project's needs. Approximately 80% of the new construction and addition projects our firm encounters have some sort of site condition, which becomes a governing factor in the overall design, budget, and timeline. I'm not sharing this to scare you out of building your dream building. I want to make certain you are able to make an educated, and professionally guided, decision towards selecting the best piece of property to fit your needs.

So here is an idea: Why not do some homework prior to signing on the dotted line in the closing room? Savvy developers, and large conglomerates, know no piece of land is perfect and there will be issues. For the buyer, the goal is to minimize these issues and be very strategic about their selection. This knowledge and methodology is not just for those purchasing very large parcels; it is applicable for even the smallest of lots. Why not utilize this process and save money, time, and stress in the future?

The following chapters will take you through just a few of the obstacles that have been encountered by many. I will attempt to help you steer clear of these impediments. Some suggestions may be applicable, others may not, but the goal is to become highly familiar with your potential property, and look past the panoramic view to really see what you are purchasing. In many cases, some light research may be all that is needed to check a few possible lots off of your list; while other times it will take some professional consulting and testing to determine the feasibility of the future structure on that particular lot. I cannot stress enough that bringing on a team of professionals to help with this process will be highly beneficial and cost effective in the long run.

Prior knowledge regarding the soil conditions, covenants, and development requirements in the area is what this team will bring to the table, as well as the capability of providing insight as to what you are going to be tied to for a very long time.

The development and building process should be fun. It is a vision brought to fruition, which is extremely satisfying. While no construction process is problem free, utilizing these tools will take much of the frustration out of the process and enable you to go into the journey with clear expectations, and enjoy the view, brick by brick.

Boundary Issues

Surveys, Easements, and Encroachments

"What do you mean I can't put anything on that 50' portion of my property? And why do I have to maintain it if the utility company won't let me develop it? So if they bring their trucks in to service the lines, I get stuck with any damage they do to the sod or landscape material? Then why am I paying a mortgage and taxes on that swatch of land?" All good questions, and unfortunately, I hear them often.

Most property transactions require a survey in order to determine the metes and bounds, or dimensions and directions of the limits of the property, as well as any easements or adjacent property encroachments that may exist. Unfortunately, few real estate agents, or surveying professionals, take the time to explain just what is on the survey. This vital paperwork gets shoved into the closing packet folder, never again to see the light of day until your design professional, or a building official, requests a copy to verify your parcel limits.

Upon digging this piece of paper out of a box under your bed, you present it only to find out that your neighbor has built a structure, placed a driveway, or erected a fence on your property. No doubt a very uncomfortable discussion is in your near future with that neighbor. Unfortunately, you must live next to them for years after this conversation. Conversely, the survey reveals there are improvements on your parcel that extend over the property line onto your neighbor's property. It does not matter that you may not have been the one that placed it there. You now "own" the issue, and it is up to you to remedy it. In some cases, the neighbor may allow some limited encroachment, but in other cases, the improvement must be removed at your expense. Setbacks will be required, and followed, in rebuilding the improvement, which may prevent the reconstruction of the element altogether. We will discuss setbacks in more detail in a later chapter.

Other issues that may be revealed by the survey, are existing easements which could be remnants of old right of ways, access roads, or utility access easements. In the case of the old right of ways, there are ways to request these be removed, but this takes time and additional funds, and must be reviewed, and approved, by the jurisdiction having authority in your area. Access roads are a bit more complicated as these may connect landlocked properties with main roads, thus making part of your property the driveway, or a secondary road, for access to this parcel. And guess what? You get to maintain this road and pay taxes on it! There are times these easements can be negotiated to be moved, but once again, this takes time, money, and tact since you are dealing with another property owner who will be your neighbor. As for easements, just be prepared to keep those areas free of any built structures, and open to use by others, which can greatly limit the development of your property.

So how do you know about these issues prior to sitting down at the closing table? Request to have the survey completed, and in your hands, <u>prior</u> to closing, Do not be afraid to ask the realtor, surveyor, or your design professional for an explanation of the survey. Ask about encroachments and, ask about any easements that exist on the parcel. These are pertinent questions that can aid you in making a decision about the purchase of the property. Don't be afraid to walk away from a parcel that does not meet your needs, will cost more money to correct encroachment issues, or that will stifle the development of the parcel. There are many other options you have available to you.

Unseen Opportunities Or Constraints

Zoning: Setbacks, Height Restrictions, and Coverage

A client of mine put a piece of property, with a view of the Gulf of Mexico, under contract for purchase. It was a large parcel that appeared to have ample acreage, frontage on a busy thoroughfare, and plenty of tourist traffic to patron the intended restaurant, hotel, and spa. The front two parcels were zoned tourist commercial, which allowed a specific height, setbacks, and lot coverage. The parcels towards the Gulf were zoned tourist residential, which allowed the same height, but had greater setbacks, and less lot coverage. The project was designed with the hotel, spa, and restaurant on the tourist commercial portion of the lot, and the parking, amenity package, and some condominium units were located within the tourist residential portion. It was a beautiful design that tiered down to human and residential scale in height, allowed views of the water, and treated the elevated parking element such that you could not tell it wasn't part of the aesthetically pleasing building. Seems cut and dry, right? Hardly!

The purchase price of the parcels and construction costs had to be covered by the amount of revenue from the condominiums and hotel rooms. However, once the parking was put on the site, setbacks implemented, lot coverage calculated, and height restrictions complied with, the required room counts to make the project work were lacking. To add to this rather large issue, the parking garage was not allowed in the tourist residential zoning, even though the entire bank of parcels were once designated as a PUD (Planned Unit Development.) There was no way to cram the commercial uses and the parking garage on the two front parcels, so the client had to apply for a land-use change. Although the project was still viable, it took its toll in the form of time, money, and frustration.

Did the realtor disclose the zoning? Completely. Were the development standards set forth by the local authorities available to the client for review and contemplation? Absolutely. Did the client get a design professional involved prior to signing on the dotted line at the closing table to purchase the property? Totally. They did everything right that would enable them to walk away from those parcels and the development deal if the land use did not get approved.

The land use change did not go through. Can you imagine what would have happened if they had purchased the property and then tried to get the initial conceptual design work done? They would have been stuck with several very expensive parcels, without the ability to build their project due to the figures not working financially. This situation happens quite often and is completely avoidable.

Zoning is set forth by the governing jurisdiction that a particular parcel location falls under, and identifies what uses a piece of property is allowed to embody. This clusters "like uses" together, and prevents uses from being placed adjacent to other uses that may cause issues, such as a manufacturing plant being located next to a residential community. There are prohibited uses within certain zoning areas as well as allowed uses. Some rules are vague, and some require a licensed professional to make sense of them. Knowing the zoning of a parcel, prior to even looking at it, and making sure it is feasible for your development will save you time and frustration.

Setbacks vary according to property location and the zoning of the parcel. Some are set dimensions and others are a percentage of the lot depth or width.

These proportions are set forth in order to improve open spaces between lots, promote adequate natural light access to adjacent properties, as well as aid in proper air circulation around structures. Setbacks also assist in bringing the built environment back to human scale of the pedestrian, and are utilized to improve emergency vehicular access around buildings in the event of a fire, as well as to prevent the spread of fire between structures.

Height restrictions have a similar function as setbacks in that they are set forth with the intention of allowing adjacent properties access to sunlight, without building shadows blocking the light; responding to human scale, so as to not create a cavernous feeling when walking between buildings; and keeping similar heights of structures clustered in designated zoning areas to create a certain ambiance and character. The height can be measured from the finished grade to the top of roof, mean or average roof line, ceiling of uppermost habitable space, or top of uppermost built structure as outlined by the land development requirement governing the area and parcel.

Lot coverage requirements encourage clustering of built elements so that there are natural spaces and areas to soften developments; collect and treat storm water; and provide opportunities for outdoor uses. Many times the land area between the property lines and setbacks comes very close to meeting the open-space requirements.

Parcels of land look much bigger prior to subtracting portions of it for setbacks, limitations on the amount of land that can be covered, limitations on the height of any structure, and of course the required parking and storm water allocations. There have been many projects that have been limited by the amount of parking that can fit on a site. In many cases, vehicles, and the circulation space required to maneuver them on and through a site, take up more acreage than the building itself. Some developers choose to utilize a parking structure, or garage, in order to free up valuable land, but height restrictions sometimes work against this solution. Also, there must be enough space on the site to capture and treat any storm water, without it being discharged onto adjacent pieces of property owned by others, or flushed into the roadway.

Prior to purchasing a parcel, it is recommended that you determine what size of a building you would like to construct. This is where a design professional is extremely helpful, as they are able to assist in calculating the square footages and required support spaces for the building. The shape and orientation of the structure does not matter at this point, as we are just trying to get an idea of how much land may be required to support your future development. Next, calculate the amount of parking required to support the facility according to the permitting jurisdiction the parcel falls under. Your design professional can then take this parking count and determine the acreage required for parking spaces as well as the vehicular circulation needed. Based on the surface area of parking lot and building, your design professional is able to calculate the approximate size of the storm water pond, or holding area, needed. Put all of these variables together, and you have the bare minimum, buildable area you will need to make your project viable. This plan is exclusive of setbacks, easements, required open space, etc. Keep in mind that a creative design team is able to adapt a building program to a site, but there is still just so much that will fit on a site and still be permittable. This information allows you to begin looking for the correct acreage, thus saving time and eliminating sites that just don't fit your future plans.

Beauty Is Only Sod Deep

Soils, Caverns, and Aquifers

Our team was sitting in a pre-construction conference with the general contractor and his subcontractors. The agenda was followed and all seemed to be on target to begin construction on the 8,000 square foot endocrinology clinic. A voice spoke up from the corner of the conference room.

"You have soil issues," the site subcontractor said. I interjected, "The geotechnical report did not identify any poor soil conditions and the foundation system has been based on this criteria." The site subcontractor chimed in again, "I did the site work on the property next door. Believe me, you have soil issues."

This is not what you want to hear when you have permits in hand, the client has a tight timeline to occupy the new facility, and the geotechnical work and foundation system designs are done.

Information was pulled on the property next door, and sure enough, it had required extensive demucking and removal of unsuitable and organic material that would not have supported a building. But how could that property have so many hidden issues and our report not show any issues based on the soil borings. Further investigation was warranted. At this point, a different testing company was engaged to perform soil borings, and the results were shocking. We had at least 15 feet of unsuitable material to remove before even getting to a point where we could backfill with suitable soils to begin construction. This not only blew the budget, it also dissolved the timeline. The client would be required to extend his lease, at his temporary location, for another 6 months and shell out approximately $50,000.00 for the removal of the muck, and refill with clean dirt. Not fun at all. Once again, location, location, location can sometimes cost you.

Soil borings are invaluable; however, they cannot fully explain, nor detect, what is going on underneath a pretty lawn. A soil boring is a sample of the soils taken by a geotechnical company. Using a drill rig, within a small area, they determine the makeup of the different strata of the earth, as well as the existing bearing capacities, water table levels, and percolation rates of the soils.

The field sample is obtained by a technician and then taken to a laboratory for analysis. Then, a geotechnical engineer pulls the data and writes a report explaining the findings. They also make recommendations for removal of unsuitable soils, surcharging the anticipated building area to determine settlement rates, and suggest foundation design recommendations. These tasks are usually performed after the parcel is purchased and a building design is finalized. The problem is that by then, you "own" the problem. Remember, in a previous chapter, we recommended determining your buildable area on a site, as well as the size of your anticipated building prior to purchasing? Well, take that a step further and have a few soil borings done to determine what you may be faced with when constructing your building. If the current owner does not allow borings prior to putting the parcel under contract, then put the purchase under contract, but contingent on performing soil testing and finding suitable soils for the project. If the soils come back as unsuitable, but you still want to purchase the parcel, that is fine; however, you will have an idea of the amount of time, and money, you will be looking at prior to putting the first pour of concrete in the ground. This allows you time to plan for the project, and a few thousand dollars spent at this point could save you upwards of fifty thousand dollars later.

Obtaining proper soil boring reports will not only aid in the design of a proper foundation, but may also identify those areas which contain subsurface caverns or aquifers. I remember a church parking lot that actually seeped water up through the asphalt due to underground aquifers, yet in other portions of the lot, the asphalt caved in due to unknown caverns below. This is nothing that a whole new parking lot, with proper base material and an underground storm water piping system, couldn't solve, but it was quite expensive and exceeded the client's pre-planning budget. It is true that soil borings cannot give you the whole picture of what is going on under the surface of your land, but it can begin to expose information that could save you months, or years, of heartache and an extensive outlay of cash.

Every parcel has a story, and chances are the adjacent parcels' story isn't too far from what your potential parcel has in store for you. Take a moment to talk to your prospective neighbors. Whether residential or commercial, the building owners can tell you a lot about what they have encountered with their property. In the case of the church, it was across the street from a community college that had a development history of encountering caverns as well as clay soils. Sometimes an entire region may contain similar issues, but if at all possible, steer clear of those areas known to have hidden, or subsurface, nuances.

You Can Look, But You Can't Touch

Wetlands, Endangered Species, and Sacred Spaces

Imagine finding a piece of land that has just the right amount of acreage, is located in the vicinity desired, looks to be high and dry, and is priced to sell! A dream come true, right? Well, it is also a dream come true for that snail darter that calls the parcel home, and that just so happens to be on the endangered species list. This actually happens more often than you know. Unsuspecting buyers purchase a piece of land, develop a site plan and building concept, only to find an endangered species habitat in the middle of their development. This can bring construction to a grinding halt and force you, the land owner, to either relocate your improvements elsewhere, or find another conducive habitat for your new best friend, the snail darter. Additionally, you have to pay to have "your friends" located, caught, and transported elsewhere. After all, they were in this location first.

Another likely scenario that happens far too frequently, you fall in love with a wooded, beautiful piece of land, buy it, plan to clear portions of it to build your dream, and then receive a friendly call from the Department of Environmental Protection. You are advised you have jurisdictional wetlands on your site. Pretty to look at, but you cannot touch any of it. What? You paid for land you cannot do anything with? And you are going to have to pay taxes on it every year? Welcome to a nightmare. Now, you get to hire, and pay for, a wetland delineation survey to determine just how much of your land is jurisdictional. More expense and time is incurred. It may seem all is lost, and you will not be able to see your vision come to fruition. There are ways around this situation, such as changing your entire plan to build only in those areas that are not designated wetlands. Another option is to buy more wetlands, in the same or more endangered watershed area, and deed it over to the Department of Environmental Protection so it can forever remain wetlands. Then, they will allow you to develop on your wetlands, but not until you demuck the area and bring in suitable fill to build on. Remember the story in the previous chapter? $50,000 and six months later you are finally ready to put in a foundation. Oh, and did I mention that the of buying and deeding wetlands to the Department of Environmental Protection is not an even swap? You may have to deed over more acreage than you plan to develop. The ratios vary based on the condition of the wetlands being considered. There have been cases where the governmental official required a buyer to "enhance" an existing wetland in order to return a failing wetland to its more pristine condition.

There are other cases where property owners begin construction and discover there are burial grounds in the middle of what was to be their living room. Didn't the surveyor indicate a toppled headstone on their survey? How did this happen, and what do you do now? I have actually seen neighborhoods planned around one burial plot. It made a wonderful wooded roundabout, but forced replatting of parcels. The reality is that someone paid for that piece of land, and is paying taxes on it, but is not able to fully utilize what they purchased.

I know this sounds somewhat negative, but on the bright side, these situations are totally avoidable. There are environmental companies that perform Phase I, and site investigation studies, to determine whether there are any endangered species, wetlands, contamination, or other issues with a specific parcel.

NOT IN MY BACKYARD!

COVENANTS, DESIGN REGULATIONS, AND REVIEW BOARDS

As an architect, I am tasked with sitting on several review boards, developing covenants for new neighborhoods, and performing compliance reviews for new buildings. This is not a popular position to hold, due to the fact that many property owners have never read their covenants, have no idea there even are any covenants, and basically believe they are able to do whatever they would like on their piece of property. Unfortunately, it's up to me to tell them otherwise. This does not make me a very popular person, but it does motivate me to share this information with the person looking to purchase a piece of property, because once you buy it, you have also bought into the design regulations and covenants of that purchase. Yes, variances are sometimes granted, but this takes time, much effort, and you have to be able to justify the inquiry.

Planned communities, gated developments, and exclusive subdivisions usually come with quite a bit of "baggage" or issues. More than likely, there are covenants that govern anything that is built or improved upon. This sometimes includes such things as what type of vegetation you plant, what color you want to paint your structure, and what type of window treatments you choose to cover your windows. Covenants may seem very controlling, but these rules are in place to keep the level of appearance, and property values, of the area consistent. It is very important to ask your realtor for a copy of any covenants that govern the parcel you are considering. Too many times these covenants are introduced to the buyer at the closing table, and you have absolutely no idea what you are getting yourself into. Think you are going to build a three-story building? Nope. The covenants cap heights at two stories. It happens, trust me. Please get a copy of the covenants *prior to* buying that beautiful piece of land.

As to design regulations, they are everywhere and you live with them daily. Design regulations govern everything from signage, to mailboxes, and the amount of site coverage allowed. General building codes contain regulations, but just like an onion, you must peel back each layer to reveal another set of requirements based on location, district, overlay zones, and special treatment areas. And, just like an onion, sometimes it makes you cry. Many people don't even realize they are in these regulated zones until they receive a stop-work order, a certified letter, or a friendly visit from the building inspector. This situation is where some initial fact finding is useful prior to closing on a piece of land. Pay a visit to the local building and planning departments of your township and inquire about what covenants, regulations, and codes govern the parcel. Many times, the governing agency will point you to a website, or give you a copy of the regulations, so you are able to read it and digest the information at your leisure. Please read their information carefully. It will save you time and money. Another option is to hire a design professional who knows where to look for the information, is on a first name basis with the code officials, and can glean the pertinent requirements from all of that paperwork and explain it in layman's terms to you.

Permission to build, remodel, or renovate doesn't just come from the building department. It comes from your Property Owner's Association, as well as any special overlay, treatment, or design zone boards. I have seen businesses' signage delayed for months due to not reading the Architectural

Guidelines for historic downtown areas, which many times results in loss of revenue. Also, there have been cases of homes delayed for months due to the property owner, and designer, not realizing they must abide by covenants and regulations they have never seen, nor realized existed. That places them back to square one, and starting over on the design is not a good thing, especially when you really need to be moved in by a certain date! Fact finding and information gathering will save time, money, and unnecessary heartache.

Bad Timing

Development Order, Design, Permitting, and Construction Timelines

Timelines matter. Many of my clients come to me with very tight development and construction schedule constraints. Whether you are planning on renovating an existing structure, building a new building, or developing a large campus, design and permitting takes quite a bit of time and can sometimes be very unpredictable. Your designer should be able to give you a design schedule that takes into account not only production of the documents, but also allows for review time by you. The closer you work with your design professional, the quicker this process progresses. Our team makes every effort to estimate the amount of time it will take to permit a project, but truth be told, there is really no way of knowing what red tape you may encounter.

When dealing with a pristine piece of land, or changing an overall site's use or lot coverage, you must permit the land first. This may require that you obtain permits from the Department of Environmental Protection, as well as a development order from the local governing authority. Areas of concern for regulatory agencies to consider when reviewing your development applications are usually the anticipated building area and placement, adequate parking, storm water drainage and retention, utility availability, capacity and connection, and compliance with setbacks and buffers. This process can sometimes take anywhere from one to twelve months for review, comments, and resubmittal processes to be completed. Even if you fully comply with all regulations, you are not ensured a quick and painless process; however, being aware of the possible delays and long timelines will enable you to plan adequately, and remain calm, even when you want to scream!

So, you have obtained your land permits, development order, and letters of compliance from the governing authorities. Don't break out the shovel yet. You still have to obtain a building permit. Review timelines vary; however, they seem to be a bit more expeditious than the development order process. I advise contacting the building department to inquire about the usual review timeframe for your project type and size, and then add a week, or two, for any glitches. Plan for the worst case scenario, and then be delighted when your permits come through within this timeframe.

Construction is a nonperfect process that takes man-made and natural materials, and must adapt in an ever-changing, outdoor environment. When you choose a contractor to erect your structure, obtain a construction schedule. The contractor will make every effort to anticipate delays and provide a realistic completion date. But, please understand that things happen. Weather happens. Material shortages happen. Lack of laborers happens. Life happens. Build in a buffer based on the project size, location, and complexity. A job well done takes time. Be patient and prepare for delays. They happen.

LET IT RAIN, LET IT RAIN, LET IT RAIN

STORM WATER

I once worked at an architectural firm that had an incredible view of the bay. To the front of the building, we had downtown rising up the hill; to the rear of the building, there was a vast expanse of scrub palms and a sandy beach. Beautiful. We parked to the side of the building and enjoyed what most would call a picturesque setting. However, when it rained, the waters came running down the hill from downtown, flooded the parking lot, and then proceeded to creep under the walls of the building, slowly and eerily rising within the building. We put the lovely, wood desks on concrete blocks, placed our computers on top of our desks, and proceeded to work as best we could. When it was time to go home, we put on our waders, if we had them with us, and prayed our cars would start due to the doors being below the water level. It didn't help that I was driving an MR2 at the time. To say this was a problem is an understatement. The issue was the office was in a flood-prone area. Another issue was there was minimal storm water management for downtown; therefore, we enjoyed the runoff from several, contiguous city blocks.

This is a common problem in existing areas that didn't have storm water regulations when the buildings were built. Water just ran where it ran, and most of the time it ran right into a neighboring parcel's acreage. We still have issues in densely populated areas, but municipalities have realized they need to build some sort of infrastructure to collect, treat, and either hold, or discharge, the storm water. This is quite an invasive and costly endeavor when a city is built out. Storm water inlets must be installed, underground piping laid, and the water has to go somewhere. Many times parcels are purchased by the municipality in order to put in a collective storm water treatment plant and holding pond. Some of these ponds are nicely landscaped with benches and decorative fencing, and include a water feature in order to move the water so it doesn't become stagnant and full of algae. Other ponds become overgrown areas that collect trash and debris, depending on available funds for maintenance, and the overall attitude of the municipality.

So what happens if the parcel you want to purchase does not have access to a collective storm water facility? You must collect and treat the storm water on your parcel. There is no sharing of your water with your neighbors; it is all yours. This is why I recommend planning your development prior to purchasing your parcel. Know how much storm water you are going to be dealing with, and have a plan for how to handle it.

First, calculate how much area you are going to cover with buildings or paving material. Then determine, from local information, how much rainfall you are anticipating. This is normally viewed as the worst case scenario, or hundred-year storm. Multiply these two numbers and you have the approximate amount of water you must put somewhere. Integrating green roofs, and rainwater collection, into your design for use in flushing toilets and irrigating landscapes, will help in reducing this volume of water. In the parking lot design, using permeable paving systems, which allow the water to seep through the paving material into the ground below, helps to more evenly disburse water into the soil. The remaining water will need to be routed, or piped, to a storm water detention, or retention pond, for treatment and eventual percolation into the ground. This takes up some acreage, and the pond's depth is determined by the volume of water, percolation rate of the soil, and amount of parcel space you are willing to allot to storm water management.

But, what happens if the soils don't absorb or percolate well? This is another reason to perform soil investigations prior to purchasing the parcel. By doing a few soil borings, a testing agency is able to tell you what the soil is made up of, how dense it is, and how well it percolates. They can also tell you how close to the surface the ground water levels, or water table, resides. If the water table is close to the surface, and you get a big storm, it doesn't matter how well the soil drains, you may have a lake to deal with.

So how do you handle storm water if the parcel has poor soil? One way is to build a pond, or several ponds, to contain the water. Chances are if the soils are subpar, the water will not percolate very quickly, and you will have a wet pond for a while. So plan on aerating the pond to keep it from being stagnant. Another option would be to amend the soils in the pond area so that they do percolate. If you do not have the acreage to build a pond, the water could be directed, collected, and stored in underground storage piping. These pipes have perforated bottoms and will allow the water to percolate slowly. This is an expensive option, but is frequently used for parcels with high intensity development. Much excavation, and laying of gravel or conducive soil beds, prior to the laying of the piping makes this option feasible only if all else fails.

Having a plan for how much of the land is going to be developed, testing the soils to determine the percolation quality and water table, as well as planning for storm water, will ensure you do not paint yourself into a corner when purchasing a parcel.

HIGH MAINTENANCE

REGULATORY MONITORING AND ACCESS

It is always smart to check into what regulatory red tape you may encounter when developing a piece of land. Will you be able to fully contain your storm water during construction as well as during the lifespan of your development? Does your parcel have any wetlands present, and are they jurisdictional? Are there any endangered species present? Are there any easements that must be kept open during construction, and that limit your use of the land? Many of these topics have been discussed earlier in this book, but it is important to understand these issues are not just a one-time inconvenience, but are forever your issue. The regulatory agencies have a right to access your property, at any time, and inspect the premises to determine if the permits are in compliance. They may also utilize the easements and you must deal with the disruption that comes with such an operation.

When you develop your site and build your building, the storm water system must be built and monitored ... forever in most cases. Different jurisdictions require different monitoring criteria for the Storm Water Quality Permit, but a storm water management plan must be written, approved by the jurisdiction having authority, and followed for the lifetime of the facility, or project. Some of the items that will be part of your management plan are: a description of the maintenance activities for the pond and a schedule of such maintenance; a description of any pesticides envisioned to be used to control vegetative growth, as well as an application schedule; and a litter control plan with a timeline for inspections, just to name a few.

The Permitee, which is you, will need to certify proper maintenance is being performed on the system, and conduct inspections, once a month, as well as after significant rain events. Some items to include in the inspection certification report are: removal of any litter or debris; identification of, and repair of, any storm water structure failures; documentation of any repairs performed, as well as identification of any standing water, the amount of rain received during a rain event; and the period of time since the last rain event. An annual report should also be generated by a licensed engineer, and filed as part of your annual renewal of your Storm Water Quality Permit. This report usually includes verification and any changes to your litter control plan, pesticides, inlet repair or maintenance, and public education practices that keep those looking after your building informed of the permit's requirements for the storm water area.

If there are mitigated wetlands on your property, you will encounter ongoing wetland monitoring as well as, more than likely, implementation of a conservation easement that will ensure no one will be able to develop that portion of land in the future. The Department of Environmental Protection actively monitors these wetlands, and will perform inspections, some of which you may not be aware are being performed. The wetland monitoring plan is intended to ensure the survival of at least 80% of the wetland vegetation, and habitat, as well as to control exotic and/or nuisance plant species, keeping these to less than 5% total wetland area coverage through specific, and intentional, monitoring and extraction activities. Monitoring of these wetlands will continue until the wetland is deemed to be thriving and functioning/building a natural habitat for vegetation and wildlife conducive and indigenous to your area and watershed.

In the event your site is home to a protected or

endangered species, you may be required to relocate the species or protect, enhance, and conserve their portion of your property. Relocation will involve a study of suitable alternate "homes" for your endangered, or protected, species which must closely match your habitat. Then a plan will be generated to trap, transport, and release the species to their new habitat. Specialty consultants, as well as the Fish and Wildlife Conservation Commission in your area, are able to assist in this process. Please do not try to do this project by yourself. Jail is not comfortable, and the fines are expensive. If you choose to share your property with the species, a habitat management plan, as well as a protected species monitoring plan, will need to be written, followed, and enforced. These plans are usually required by your local, state, and federal permitting agencies, and should involve a specialty consultant. Be prepared to allow, and perform, periodical inspections, and/or reports, for the jurisdictions having authority, so they can ensure you are indeed maintaining the habitat for your protected, or endangered, species.

Easements often accompany a piece of property after the sale, but few new owners are prepared for the periodic intrusion of those who have rights to said easement. You may feel that portion of the property is yours, and you are able to plant whatever you want and utilize the land however you want. But, if those who have rights to this easement want access to this land, or need to dig anything up within this easement, you may lose whatever you planted, as well as have to regrade, or clean up, the mess afterwards. Of course, there are some instances when those who access the easement take great care to minimize disruption, and replace anything that has been negatively altered, but in most cases, there may be rutted areas, dirt all over everywhere, and a species of sod reinstalled that was certainly not there initially. Crying won't help, screaming may, but being aware of the rights and limitations of those granted access to the easement will aid in knowing what to expect if they do exercise these rights.

Pay Their Way

Permits and Development Costs

How can a project be a money pit before you even put a shovel in the ground? Easily. Few people think about what may be required, permit wise, prior to purchasing a piece of property. Permitting should be easy, right? You get some plans drawn up, go down to the building department, and pull a permit to build your dream! Not so fast! There are many hoops to jump through prior to pulling the building permit, and plenty of fees to go along with those hoops. Depending on the "jurisdiction having authority," you may be required to pull a development order, first, to make sure the development of the site is done per zoning and code. Also, are utilities available? If not, guess who will be footing the bill to extend those electrical, water, or sewer lines to your property. That's right, you!

I have had many clients who did not inquire about utility availability prior to purchasing their parcel, and then were in sticker shock when they received the bill to extend water, sewer, gas, or electrical lines to their property. In many cases, it is not just a single service line that was required; it was an extension of the main line, and then a connection to that main. You may ask why they had to pay for the main extension. It's because they were the first to develop in that location, and the jurisdiction envisions more development in that direction; therefore, the first in line to build must pay for the main service extensions. Your future neighbors will thank you for paying their way by putting these lines in, and picking up the tab. Many times these lines are quite large and can be costly. The jurisdiction may agree to pay for the line extension, or a portion thereof, but you should inquire prior to buying the parcel.

You may be telling yourself that you will just dig a well, or put in a septic tank, in lieu of hooking into, or extending services, to your parcel. Be careful and ask questions, because there are situations where the jurisdiction requires you to hook up to their services in order to develop the land. There is a connection fee that is based on the number of plumbing fixtures in your building, or the size of your facility. If the available service is not adequate to handle your additional load, guess who gets to pay for the size increase in the main lines, or to put in a booster pump? Yes, you, and remember: a shovel has yet to hit the ground.

Another item reviewed in the development order process is vehicular traffic flow and control. A traffic study is often required in more urban areas to determine the amount of increased vehicular use your development will cause for existing roadways. If your "trips," which are how many times a vehicle leaves and returns to your property, increase congestion and traffic significantly, you may be required to put in a turn lane, deceleration lane, traffic light, cross walk, or widen the whole roadway. So, if you thought extending utilities was expensive, try widening roads and putting in traffic signals. There have been some developments that had significant limitations to their site access to the point of having to drive past their property, turn around and then drive the other way in order to pull into a "right in, right out" curb cut. This happens quite frequently, especially if the parcel is located near an intersection. Crossing traffic in these locations is not easy, and in some cases, not allowed. How can this be avoided? Some due diligence, and a discussion with a civil engineer who is familiar with your type of development and the local jurisdictions, should shed some light on what may be required. There are situations where the development requirements cannot be determined until you have your design, and the traffic studies are performed, but at least you know you will have those costs to incur. Also, do not forget to build the study into your development timeline, as well as review and analysis time by your jurisdiction, or the Department of Transportation. If you are on a tight timeframe, you may want to give some parcels a second thought or keep looking for another location.

Can't Get There From Here

Site Access and Utility Availability

In the previous chapter, I briefly went over the scenario of the location of your parcel in relation to existing curb cuts, intersections, and the possible requirement of having to put in deceleration lanes, turn lanes, traffic signals, and cross walks. This is a perfect segway into the "You Can't Get There From Here" chapter. Have you ever tried to get somewhere only to realize the traffic patterns, layouts, and the building location completely were working against you to the point of frustration, colorful language, and eventual relinquishing the desire to go to that destination at all! I have been this frustrated more than once! Many believe that location, location, location is all you need to gain large walk-in traffic and exposure to the general market. This is not always the case in the above described parcels. Many times, buildings very close to an intersection are the toughest to gain access to, especially from a busy road, due to medians, as well as traffic management structures, that are meant to streamline the circulation, but only create chaos. If you are a business, this is not good for your clientele. I have seen great businesses, with a devoted following, fail due to patrons not being able to easily gain access. Spend a bit of time, prior to buying a parcel, traveling different routes to the site, during peak and slow traffic flow times, in order to truly understand what your clients will experience in trying to get to you. This may change your decision on location, location, location.

I witnessed another business, which chose to locate their facility just a few feet off of a main road, only to find they could not adequately locate signage so they could be seen from the main road. If you are a destination, this is not a real problem, but if you are a business that benefits from drive-by traffic, this is a huge problem! The business didn't realize this problem until it was too late. Parcel bought, building built, and no one knows where they are located. Oops. What could have been done to prevent this? A bit of research and the occasional drive-by may have given a clue.

Let's say your goal is to locate in a rather remote, or less urban, area. The peace and quiet, low traffic, and country living is appealing. However, please do your homework about what may be available as far as utilities and services. Can you get there from here? Your county, or city, entities may not provide you with roadways, so you may have to pave, or grade, your own access road and driveway. This could be a very expensive endeavor. In addition, you may also be responsible for the maintenance of said roadway over the years, and after storms. Are you able to get power, water, and sewer service? Are you allowed to put in a well or septic system? If you are not able to connect to services, or put in your own, you may not be permitted to build a building on the parcel without incurring major development costs. Asking these questions, and developing a game plan prior to purchasing your land, will enable you to make sure you have the funds and time to do what you envision.

Conclusion

It is my sincere hope that this book has not scared you, but instead enlightened you as to the opportunities, and pitfalls, to selecting and purchasing the right parcel of land for you. It is a lifelong dream of many people to be able to build their own home, or business, from the ground up, and see their vision come to fruition. I want this outcome for you, as well, but done in a manner that protects you, and gives you realistic expectations of what you will be facing in the process. Engage professionals to help you through the process. This will save you time, money, and heartache in the future. We have developed a short checklist that will aid in obtaining, and keeping track of, your findings on the parcels that are being considered. You are able access this checklist on our website, vbadesign.us.

Some realtors, or owners, may not cooperate in helping you do your due diligence, but there are others who want good things for you, and are willing to help you in selecting the right piece of land. Seek these professionals out, and keep them close, as they will become good friends and then you will want to refer them to others. As mentioned, the contents of this book are not an all-inclusive list of items to verify, but they will help keep you from buying a nightmare instead of a dream. Ask questions, do your homework, get help when needed, and know our team wants nothing more than for you to walk into your new building with a sparkle in your eye, a smile on your face, and hear you say, with a sigh, "This is exactly what I always dreamed of!"